RULES
OF THE
GAME

HOW TO WIN A JOB
IN EDUCATIONAL LEADERSHIP

THE WORKBOOK

MARILOU RYDER, ED.D

Rules of the Game: How to Win a Job in Educational Leadership Workbook

©2019 Dr. Marilou Ryder

ISBN: 978-0-9904103-4-8

Library of Congress Control Number: 2019903830

DELMAR PUBLISHING
Huntington Beach, CA 92648

Printed in the United States of America

Contents

How to Use this Workbook   1

The Score Card   3

Recommendations and References   9

Letters of Introduction   11

RESUMES: Creating a Tagline   16

RESUMES: Writing an Accomplishment   19

Writing Your Resume   22

Interviewing: The Opening Question   27

Interviewing: The "Real You"   29

Interviewing: Scrimmage Notes   31

Perfecting Your Brand   43

Final Exam   48

APPENDIX   53

Sample Resume   54

Sample Interview Questions for Educational Leaders   58

Resume Power Words   62

Final Exam Answer Key   65

Worthy Career Websites   66

How to Use this Workbook

This workbook is to be used as a resource guide in companion with the book, *Rules of the Game: How to Win a Job in Educational Leadership.* I strongly encourage you to read the book before embarking on the activities in this workbook.

One of the most important aspects of gaining a new position of leadership is to enhance the five main tenets that comprise what I like to call your "Promotion Quotient". If you take time to plan, package yourself, prepare for the interview, persevere when you just don't think you can interview one more time, and continue to update your brand then you will have all the tools for moving ahead.

Follow each one of the "GAME TACTICS" presented throughout this workbook to help you become more familiar with the various components of gaining a new position of educational leadership. Spend time with each exercise by filling in all the answers to each section. Know that by writing down your answers, you are also adding to your collective memory to support questions that may come up in the high stakes job interview. Write it down, commit it to memory. Good luck on your new journey. I am confident since you purchased this workbook that you are now ready to do what it takes to move to the next level in your career.

Promotion Quotient

Planning
Packaging
Preparing
Persevering
Perfecting Your Brand

Career Goals
Resume
Letter of Introduction
References
Interviewing Skills
Mentors and Sponsors
Professional Brand Awareness

The Score Card

GAME TACTIC

Moving up to the next level in your career is not an easy task and you need to be ready. Every author will make necessary assumptions about his or her audience when writing a book. When writing this book, I made the following assumptions:

- You are ambitious and competitive.

- You are a high performer in your field.

- You are considering career advancement.

- You have colleagues in the field but do not have a designated mentor.

- You are working on a resume and cover letter, but want to refine them.

- You will do what it takes to attain your goals.

Do any of the above bullets strike a chord? If so, get out your yellow highlighter and sticky notes—and let's get to work on this project!

GAME TACTIC

Before you set out on your path, take this short quiz that asks a few personal and professional questions. After you complete the assessment target 3-4 specific areas to target as your personal challenges.

YOUR SCORE CARD

Yes	No		
		1.	Do you have a long term career plan in place relative to your educational leadership goals?
		2.	Are you being granted interviews when applying for advanced positons of leadership?
		3.	Does your cover letter and resume stand out in the crowd and show paper screeners you're ready for the job?
		4.	Are you aware of the wide range of questions asked in interviews?
		5.	Have you been preparing in advance for the wide range of questions asked in an interview?
		6.	Are you prepared for the challenges of the high stakes interview environment?
		7.	Have you come in second after an interview for a job?
		8.	Do you have someone you can talk to that is knowledgeable about job search particulars?
		9.	Do you know how to inform your immediate supervisors about your plans to move up?
		10.	Do you know how to ask for recommendations from key people?
		11.	Do you know how to inject purpose and humor into the interview?

FOCUS AREAS

Highlight two or three areas that you intend to focus on.

1.

2.

3.

Developing Your Career Plan

GAME TACTIC

The wise quote, "Fail to plan, plan to fail" reminds us of the importance of setting goals, strategies to achieve those goals, and action steps to get things done. As educators, we are constantly planning our next event, meeting, project, or academic achievement. We almost do this without thinking. If you are a successful planner you will ultimately become a successful administrator and your planning efforts will help you deal with the unexpected that inevitably occurs.

Some people decide to become administrators overnight, without much thought or planning. They comb through job openings and fill out application forms, with the dream of moving on and picking up a bigger paycheck. These applicants often end up frustrated or embarrassed, as they find themselves unprepared to deal with questions asked in high stakes interviews. You may choose to begin your journey that way—but trust me, this strategy is not rewarding.

GAME TACTIC

Take some time on the next activity to write down your current job and then reflect on where you see yourself in the future. Project ahead and chart out where you would like to be over the next ten years.

DEVELOPING YOUR CAREER PLAN

Position	Year(s)	Location/Type of District
Past:		
Past:		
Past:		
Current:		
Projected:		
Projected:		
Projected:		

LONG TERM ULTIMATE CAREER GOAL

Write a sentence about where you imagine yourself at the end of your career. Be bold!

GAME TACTIC

Working With Mentors and Sponsors

If you want to increase your chances for job promotions, it's essential to work with selected mentors and sponsors. Don't be afraid to take a chance and ask someone you trust to serve as your mentor. Most of us remember the hurdles we jumped through to gain our current jobs and remain successful, and many of us are enthusiastic about helping our colleagues. But again, you can't get help if you don't ask. Although asking for help is hard for some, it may be the most important step you will take on your journey to grow as a leader.

Finding a sponsor is another matter. Every leader needs a sponsor, a person to promote and speak well of them in public. A sponsor is the person in your corner who says things like, "Our new HR director is amazing; I worked with her on the last project and she gets things done." Another sponsor remark might sound like, "Jann is the best manager for our department. It won't be long before she's our next CEO."

Sponsors are people who support your initiatives and promote your projects. One thing, however, is that you cannot ask someone to be your sponsor. They choose you. They advocate on your behalf, often having the ability to connect you to important players and jobs. In doing so, they make themselves look good. And precisely because sponsors take a risk with you, they expect you to be a star performer and extremely loyal to them.

Sponsors know who you are and what you stand for because you have taken the time to get to know them and keep them apprised of your latest projects and accomplishments. A sponsor is someone who will go to bat for you, and wouldn't necessarily be your friend, but rather someone you admire on a professional level. As a leader consider both men and women you can tap as mentors and sponsors to help you grow, learn and thrive in your career.

GAME TACTIC

Use the following activity to make an assessment of the current mentors and sponsors in your life. Then chart out some specific strategies for engaging mentors and sponsors to guide your career success.

MENTORS AND SPONSORS

MENTORS	Strategies
Names of current mentors	To gain additional mentors
1.	1.
2.	2.
3.	3.
4.	4.
SPONSORS	**Strategies**
Names of current sponsors	To gain additional sponsors
1.	1.
2.	2.
3.	3.
4.	4.

Recommendations and References

GAME TACTIC

The terms "recommendation letter" and "reference letter" are often thought as one; however, there are real differences between the two terms.

Letters of recommendation are very specific in nature and are always addressed to a specific individual. They are written for a specific job category, usually written by supervisors. Letters of recommendation are the letters requested in most job applications.

Letters of reference are more general in nature and are usually addressed, "To Whom It May Concern." Throughout your career, it is important to ask individuals who have worked with you to write a letter of reference. For example, if you attended graduate school, ask the dean to write a letter, commenting on your performance and initiative. Also ask board members from various districts you have worked in to write you general letters of reference for your portfolio.

When requesting letters of recommendation or reference offer to send your reference people a brief list of your accomplishments and work history. Do this through email, or send them a copy of your resume.

If you have exceptionally good letters from your supervisors, a letter from a good colleague, parent or student can add another positive dimension to your application. A superintendent friend recently shared that a deciding factor for his last hire was based on a heartfelt note written by a student for him when he was a teacher.

GAME TACTIC

Complete the following activity to make an assessment of your current portfolio. As you review letters currently in your possession give each one a grade of A-F. Try to make sure that each one of your letters that you choose to use is in the A-B range if possible.

RECOMMENDATIONS AND REFERENCES

Recommendations [Name]	Check if you possess it	Assign a grade
1.		
2.		
3.		
4.		
5.		

References [Name]	Check if you have permission	Assign a grade
1.		
2.		
3.		
4.		
5.		

GAME TACTIC

Letters of Introduction

Most school districts require candidates to submit a letter of introduction (sometimes called letter of intent or cover letter) stating why they are interested in the position, qualifications and intent to officially apply to the district. This letter is extremely important and is used in educational administration to determine an applicant's personality as well as their credentials.

More importantly, the letter of introduction is an opportunity to quickly introduce yourself and catch the employer's attention. Much like the resume, it's another opportunity to market your skills to the screening committee, encourage them to read your resume, and grant you a job interview. Employers use the letter to also gain an understanding of how you write, think, and organize your thoughts. So take time when composing this letter, and do some homework on the district or position, before writing the letter.

GAME TACTIC

Review the sample letter of introduction. You don't want to copy this letter but rather use it as a guide for how to craft out your own letter. A sample template is included for you to use as a starting point.

SAMPLE LETTER OF INTRODUCTION

Dear,

Please accept this letter as an application for the position of superintendent for Sunny Valley Union High School District. I am currently serving as the superintendent of California Unified School District, one of the largest unified school districts (ADA 14,500) in the San Joaquin Valley. I am looking for a new challenge in my career and believe my strengths and skills are a perfect match of those required for the superintendent of Sunny Valley Union High School District.

My experiences in education have been wide and diverse. I have worked in five school districts and two states, gaining a breadth of experience from my involvement with many multi-cultural populations and socio-economic groups. My experiences have included classroom teaching and site administration as well serving at the district level as assistant superintendent of educational services and currently as district superintendent.

I am confident that my experiences as a superintendent can transition easily to Sunny Valley Union. My immediate goal will be to assess and validate identified strengths within the district while working with all stakeholders to set a strategic agenda for a new level of excellence.

Highlights of my educational career include:

- **Student Achievement:** Significantly improved student achievement in three school districts through the implementation of Professional Learning Communities, data driven instruction, and best practices in education.

- **Strategic Planning**: Created the first district Strategic Change Portfolio for California USD and secured unanimous agreement from key constituencies to work on four strategic initiatives. Implemented the guiding principles from Collin's Good to Great as a framework for district wide improvement.

- **High School Reform**: Led the process for a High School Quality Design Team which met to engage in research-based high school reform efforts. Nine initiatives were charted as key areas of reform.

- **Student Engagement:** Implemented a district student attendance program, *EveryDay Counts*, increasing student attendance from 95% to 97%. District revenue increased approximately $1 million while students gained over 83,500 additional hours of classroom instruction in one year. Developed Project 720 *(720 days of school in 9-12)* an intervention program that identifies potential 9th grade drop outs.

- **Relationships:** Gained the respect and trust of CSEA, CTA, parents and students through honest and open communication venues that included formal advisory councils.

- **Resource Management and Facilities:** 1) successfully monitored a $110 million district budget which currently supports a 5% reserve; (2) responsible for the passage of Measure B, a $152 million general obligation bond, supported by 64% of California USD citizens; and (3) monitored construction of a football stadium, transportation facility and new elementary school.

- **Board Relations:** Successfully improved board governance structures and facilitated agenda items that involved conscientious discussion and allowed for all viewpoints to be heard (i.e. hiring of relatives, transportation schedules, school boundaries, dress policy, naming of new schools).

I am well known for my effective people skills as evidenced by strengths in developing mutual trust and respect, sharing information through open communication systems, and recognizing and rewarding contributions toward success. Throughout my career, I have demonstrated integrity and honesty in addition to maintaining a sense of humor so often required for today's school superintendents to lead our schools.

My planning skills are well developed.

I plan with the end goal in mind and know how to bring people together to solve complex problems. I strongly believe in collaborative problem solving for negotiations as well as critical long-term district decisions.

I believe passionately in public education.

As an advocate for children and students, I believe that everyone involved with schools... everyone... must work together to ensure excellence in teaching and learning. Our children deserve no less. Thank you.

Sincerely,

Marilou Ryder, Ed. D.

LETTER OF INTRODUCTION TEMPLATE

Dear_____,

Please accept this letter as an application for the position of _____ for _____ School District. I am currently serving as the _____ of _____ School District, **[Say something positive here to describe your current district]**. I am looking for a new challenge in my career and believe my strengths and skills are a perfect match of those required for the _____ of _____ School District.

My experiences in education have been wide and diverse. **[Talk about your experience]**. _____

_____

_____

_____

I am confident that my experiences as _____ can transition easily to _____. My immediate goal will be to assess and validate identified strengths within the district while working with all stakeholders to set a strategic agenda for a new level of excellence.

Highlights of my educational career include: **[Select a few of these categories and write a recent accomplishment for each area. Do not use all of these examples and consider writing some of your own categories]**.

- Student Achievement

- Strategic Planning

- Student Engagement

- Public Engagement

- Relationships

- Resource Management and Facilities

- Board Relations

- Negotiations

- Technology

[Write a short closing statement that tells the reader what you believe in and how passionate you are about children and education].

_____

_____

_____

_____

_____

_____

_____

_____

_____

_____

_____

_____

GAME TACTIC

RESUMES:
Creating a Tagline

In today's world, we all need a powerful resume. The game is played inside. You must get through the door. I can't stress this fact enough with educators: The resume is a tool with one specific purpose—to gain entry to the interview. A resume is an advertisement; nothing more, nothing less.

An effective resume should read a lot like a great advertisement. Typically, an advertisement is created to convince you that, if you buy a particular product, you will get these specific, direct benefits. Your resume must present you in the best light and should convince the employer you have what it takes to be successful and how the district will benefit from what you have to offer.

Write your resume to create *interest*, to persuade the employer to call you. If you write with that goal in mind, your final product will be very different than if you write just to inform or catalog your job history.

To begin with, create a tagline, stating your expertise.

"What's a *tagline*?" you ask. Taglines are also known as "objectives" and are commonly used by educators in their resumes. In my opinion, taglines that are written as objectives are out-of-style. Focus your tagline in a way that makes you stand out among other applicants.

Whether marketing a new business, a book, doughnuts, or yourself, as a job candidate, the goal is to sell the product. In a job search, you are selling yourself in a very competitive market, to a very specific clientele. What is it that makes you stand out above your competition? Why are you a better candidate?

Here's an example of a tagline used in a superintendent resume:

> Student focused leader with a strong record of success. Recognized for developing mutual trust and respect, building collaborative teams, public speaking, and sharing information through open communication.

Here's another tagline used for a high school principal position:

> Accomplished instructional leader known for being an energetic and caring professional. Proven record for building high functioning teams and working through sensitive issues with positive results. A collaborative decision maker and master working under pressure.

Here's a different format for a tagline used on a superintendent resume:

STRENGTHS

Relationships - Quickly established loyal and trusting relationships with key district stakeholders.

Raising Student Achievement - Provided leadership for raising test scores in three school districts.

Revenue Enhancement - Responsible for balanced budget ending with a 12% reserve, with no layoffs.

GAME TACTIC

Complete the following exercise to develop your own Tagline. You can use this for your resume AND when you first introduce yourself in the interview.

CREATE A RESUME TAGLINE

List 2-3 of your Technical Skills (Planning, Budget, Instruction, etc.)	List 2-3 of your Soft Skills (Creativity, Communication, etc.)

Write a few words about your educational philosophy

Write a draft resume tagline

GAME TACTIC

RESUMES:
Writing an Accomplishment

Cool resume design and engaging taglines grab attention, but resume *content* is what finally sells the reader. Too many resumes that come across my desk list the person's job classification, followed by job duties. I advise my clients, "We all know what the role of an assistant principal entails—why are you telling us this?"

Rather, spend valuable white paper, telling the reader what you have done in your role to make a difference and why your performance is better than others. Go beyond showing what is required, and demonstrate how you make a difference. Provide specific examples. Ask yourself the following questions:

1. How do you perform better than others?

2. What are some problems or challenges faced and how did you overcome them?

3. Have you receive any awards or recognition as a result?

GAME TACTIC

Review the sample accomplishments that follows. Think of a program or project you have been involved with over the past two years. Write it as an accomplishment using power words and data that would reflect success. Then take some time to write 3-4 additional accomplishments that you can use on your resume.

WRITING AN ACCOMPLISHMENT

SAMPLE ACCOMPLISHMENTS

- Launched Sunny Valley Virtual High School to meet the needs of parents and students in the 21st century. This flexible district learning program provides all the academic courses offered in a traditional setting including CSU/UC approved A-G and AP courses.

- Implemented *EveryDay Counts*, a district attendance program, increasing student attendance from 95 % to 96%. District revenue increased approximately $1 million while students gained over 83,500 additional hours of classroom instruction in one year.

- Established a successful Aspiring Administrators Symposium for 75 California USD teachers and authored a corresponding article to promote the success of the program (Leadership Magazine, September, 2016). Ten participants were later hired as administrators.

Think of a program or project that you have been involved with over the past two years. Write it as an accomplishment. Try to use power words and if possible use data that would reflect positive success.

_____

_____

_____

_____

_____

_____

_____

_____

ADDITIONAL ACCOMPLISHMENTS

1.

2.

3.

4.

GAME TACTIC

Writing Your Resume

Writing or revising one's resume can be a daunting task. Get a cup of coffee, set up your computer, and get to work. Follow these simple tricks of the trade to get you off the starting block.

1. Check out a few sample resume books to get ideas.

2. Pick a design template from Word or a similar program, or develop one on your own. Begin with your name and pertinent information at the top.

3. Arrange your categories in a fashion that makes sense to you, and prioritize according to their importance. Collate the important information within each category.

4. Write to your audience. How will your experience, skills and degrees fulfill the requirements of the new job? Show how your experiences from your last job will be valuable to the one you are applying for. If you are a teacher, try to showcase your leadership experience from the classroom, and align it to experience that would be desirable as an assistant principal. For example, avoid writing: "Worked with grade level teachers to develop a job fair." Turn your grade level experience into something more powerful, such as: "Provided leadership at the site level for our sixth grade job fair."

5. Now go back and edit. Tighten up your writing to keep it concise and action-oriented to focus on your accomplishments and responsibilities. You don't have to use complete sentences—bulleted lists are best.

6. Set your first draft down on a table, walk away for a few minutes, and then come back and glance at the front page. Does the formatting grab your attention, or is it just ho-hum? Think about

formatting the document, so that it's graphically appealing. Do your headings jump out? Are fonts in synch? Work on this, until you feel you have a reader friendly document that is visually pleasing. Eliminate small type and long, rambling sentences.

7. Ask a few people to proofread, and then review it again yourself. Read each sentence in reverse for typos or words out of place.

8. Save your document in several places, and be prepared to tweak your resume to address the specific skills each school district requests.

WINNING PLAYS FOR RESUMES

Tip 1: Use an impressive design that grabs attention.

Tip 2: Create a tagline, stating your expertise.

Tip 3: Create content that sells the benefit of your skills.

Tip 4: Use Power Words.

Tip 5: Include relevant professional information.

Tip 6: Identify and solve employer needs.

Tip 7: Prioritize the content of your resume.

Tip 8: Avoid personal pronouns and articles.

Tip 9: Don't list irrelevant information.

Tip 10: No typos!

GAME TACTIC

Review the sample Resume Template that follows. Begin to fill in areas that will add depth and meaning to your resume. Remember, do not list job duties, rather draft out major accomplishments for each job held.

SAMPLE RESUME TEMPLATE

JOHN N. GREEN

4260 N. Black Ave ◆ Irvine, California 92639 ◆ 714-392-7769 ◆ jgreen@gmail.com

Leadership Qualifications

The Tagline: Write something here about your years of experience, skills and what you are known for in 2-3 sentences. This header is important. Example: Dedicated educational administrator with over xxx years' experience. Solid track record as evidenced by ability to.....

Leadership Experience

PRINCIPAL 2012-present

Hill Top High School
California Unified School District, Irvine, CA

*Use this space under each job held to highlight your accomplishments. Try to quantify when appropriate. Say things like "90% of students exceeded", etc. State from a leadership purview. List each accomplishment under each job you have held. Note some **sample** verbs. Begin each bullet with a strong VERB within the first two words. These are launch points for you to use when writing your accomplishments.*

- Significantly improved
- Developed
- Successfully launched
- Responsible for implementing
- Played integral role at the district level
- Worked alongside the superintendent
- Collaborated
- Implemented
- Participated in
- Served as a key member

ASSISTANT PRINCIPAL 2006-2012

North High School
Cerritos Union High School District, Cerritos, CA

Do the same thing here but with each job held list <u>fewer and fewer</u> accomplishments (most of your accomplishments should be from your current position.

- Provided
- Significantly improved
- Worked with all stakeholders
- Directly responsible for
- Developed
- Fine-tuned
- Created
- Spearheaded

Teaching Experience

TEACHER AND HEAD FOOTBAL COACH 1998-2006

Ontario High School

Ontario Union High School District, Ontario, CA

- Managed
- Supervised
- Oversaw
- Worked with

RESOURCE SPECIALIST- 1990-1998

Ontario High School

Ontario Union High School District, Ontario, CA

- Managed
- Created
- Developed

Education

California University 1995

Graduate studies in Special Education and Educational Administration

Claremont University, California 1990

Master of Science, Counseling and Guidance

California State University, Fresno 1989

Bachelor of Arts, Industrial Technology

Credentials

California Clear Administrative Services Credential

California Clear Pupil Personnel Services Credential

California Clear Secondary Teaching Credential
Social Studies, Industrial Technology, Special Education and Resource Specialist

Additional Professional Training

WASC Visitation Training

Accelerating the Achievement of English Learners. Conference, FCOE

Exemplary Practices In Ed. Leadership Conference. Doug Reeves

California League of High Schools: Accelerating Student Achievement. Marzano

Professional Learning Communities at Work. Rick DuFour. FCOE

Verify Students Are Learning. Data Works. John Hollingsworth

California League of High Schools: Rick DuFour PLC Conference

Getting Serious About School Reform. Robert Marzano Institute

Activities/Professional Associations

Association of California School Administrators (ASCA)

Association for Supervision and Curriculum

Principal's Partnership

Honors and Awards
Presentations and Staff Development

References (List with name, title, and telephone number)

John Jones	Barbara Smith
Superintendent	School Board Member
California School District	Cerritos School District
760-900-0556	878-666-1245
Richard Smith	Susan Peterson
Assistant Superintendent	Director of Human Resources
California School District	Ontario USD
652-999-8767	900-888-7777

GAME TACTIC

Interviewing: The Opening Question

Before or just after the first question is asked, take a moment to thank the panel. It can sound something like this:

I would like to take this opportunity to thank you for granting me an interview today. I am happy to be here and look forward to getting to know you better. Thank you.

This short exchange eases the transition between you sitting there and the onslaught of questions headed your way. It also affords you the opportunity to catch your breath and gain your composure. *Don't forget this important strategy.*

The first question, standard in the industry, takes a variety of forms but is designed to determine why you want the job, who you are, and why you think you're right for the position. That's a lot to ask in one question. This question doesn't vary much from assistant principal to superintendent, so it pays to prepare your answer in advance.

Practice your response, over and over, in front of a mirror and with friends, until you feel comfortable with what you are saying. Don't memorize your answer, but learn how to navigate through this first question. It's not an invitation to ramble, nor is it time to recite your resume.

Don't take off on where you went to grad school, or repeat your employment history. Panel members have read your resume and want more details from this question.

The first question is not one that can be answered effectively off the cuff. *I strongly advise you to take time in advance*, and think about yourself and key aspects of your personality and/or background that you want to promote or feature, during this critical opening question. This is your time to shine, and make a positive first impression.

Practice organizing your thoughts by completing this sample exercise.

OPENING STATEMENT

List three personal qualities	List three skills you bring to the position
1.	1.
2.	2.
3.	3.

Why do you want to work for this new district or take on this new job?

1.

2.

3.

Tell us a little about yourself, what qualifications you have for this position and why you want to work for us. After writing some sample ideas below, ask a close colleague to listen to your statement and ask them for critical feedback.

1.

2.

3.

Interviewing: The "Real You"

GAME TACTIC

As you may know, interviewing for a job can be very stressful. You are asked a lot of technical questions, and panel members are trying to determine if (1) you are qualified for the job, (2) have the ability to provide leadership, (3) are trustworthy, and (4) if they like you. They commonly ask themselves during the interview, "Is this a person we would like to work with? Would this person be a good team member?"

Unless you have nerves of steel and an exceptional stage presence, letting people on the panel get to know the "real you" can be a challenge. For this reason, I advise you to develop one or two human-interest stories about something in your professional or personal life that you can pull out at a moment's notice and share with the interview panel during an appropriate question.

GAME TACTIC

Begin drafting a few ideas that could be woven into a story that would show an interview panel you have "heart" and are in the profession for all the right reasons.

WHAT'S YOUR STORY?

Check any areas you believe would link your personal story to a specific interview question. Add other ideas in the unlabeled boxes.

☐ Leadership Style	☐ Communication	☐ Building Trust	☐ Problem Solving
☐ Conflict Resolution	☐ Effective Teaching	☐ Accountability	☐ Diversity
☐ At Risk Students	☐ Parents	☐ Technology	☐ Building Teams
☐	☐	☐	☐

Interviewing: Scrimmage Notes

GAME TACTIC

As an executive mentor, I like to use the word "scrimmage" as a metaphor to emphasize the most important aspect of the interview process—the practice. A scrimmage is an informal sports contest or practice match, engaged in for practice purposes, which does not count in the regular season record. [Wikipedia].

Scrimmages are not official, but atheletes try to play them like the real thing. Scrimmages are advantageous, because athletes can work out plays in advance, and get a sense for how they will play in the real game.

I have created a group of interview (scrimmage) notes to use in the preparation phase of your job search. You must be able to speak intelligently, and cite examples relative to each area. **THIS IS VERY IMPORTANT FOR YOUR SUCCESS IN THE INTERVIEW.**

The contents of each area have the potential to surface in any question. Sometimes a question can cover two areas. For example: 1) How do you use assessment to (2) improve student learning? For each area list 2-3 bullet points that you would talk about if asked a question related to that topic: For example, under the subject of teachers, in almost every interview you will be asked something about teachers. Here's some examples:

- What do you look for when you go into a teacher's classroom to determine if good instruction is taking place?

- What do you look for when hiring a teacher?

- What makes a good teacher?

Here's the strategy you can use when developing your own Scrimmage Notes. Consider the four bullet points that relate to good teachers:

TRAITS OF A GREAT TEACHER

1. Knows subject content

2. Lesson development

3. Classroom management

4. Likes kids!

If you have these bullets committed to memory, then when asked a question that relates to teachers, you can use these as a launch pad to address the question. Just know that on a good day, you will probably be able to recall and address three out of four of your bullets.

GAME TACTIC

Use the following SCRIMMAGE NOTES categories to draft out your own bullets for overarching areas related to your skill set and experience. Please remember once again, it is not effective to memorize answers to a hundred different interview questions. You do, however, need to be ready with tip-of-tongue stories and examples that substantiate your competencies, motivation, and ability to deliver results. If you have your Scrimmage Notes (bullet points) committed to memory you will be in an excellent position to speak to each question intelligently with enough time with three minutes to add a personal example or story. (Note: *Rules of The Game: How to Win a Job in Educational Leadership* provides examples you can use for each Scrimmage Note in case you need help).

SCRIMMAGE NOTES

Greatest strengths:

1.

2.

3.

Words colleagues would use to describe you:

1.

2.

3.

Improve student achievement:

1.

2.

3.

Example:

How you build trust:

1.

2.

3.

Example:

Your leadership style:

Example:

A problem and how you dealt with it:

Problem:

Solution:

Example:

Traits of a successful administrator:

1.

2.

3.

Traits of an excellent teacher:

1.

2.

3.

Navigating the change process:

1.

2.

3.

Example:

Communication:

1.

2.

3.

Example:

Decision making:

1.

2.

3.

Example:

Making people accountable:

1.

2.

3.

4.

Example:

Budget development process: (Your background and how to oversee the process.)

1

2.

3.

4.

Example:

Manage a fiscal crisis:

1.

2.

3.

4.

5.

Example:

Models of best teaching practices:

1.

2.

3.

4.

Example:

Planning skills:

1.

2.

3.

4.

Example:

ELL students:

1.

2.

3.

Example:

Partnership with community:

1.

2.

3

Example:

Save money on special education:

1.

2.

3.

Example:

Work with bargaining and unions:

1.

2.

3.

Example:

Provide for diversity:

1.

2.

3.

Example:

Involve parents:

1.

2.

3.

Example:

Lower or prevent dropouts:

1.

2.

3.

4.

Example:

Positive school or district climate:

1.

2.

3.

4.

Example:

Your greatest accomplishment:

Where will you be five years from now?:

Example:

Why hire you?:

1.

2.

3.

Hobbies, fun, etc. example:

Professional development:

1.

2.

3.

Example:

Hero/ role model example:

Last book read example:

GAME TACTIC

Perfecting Your Brand

Branding is the latest buzzword for what we used to call reputation. Professional branding communicates the essence of who you are in the workplace and reflects your professional reputation — what you're known for (or would like to be known for).* When your reputation is a good one, it includes marketable distinctions like positive characteristics and achievements. It's a way to stand out from the teeming masses of competition for the best jobs.

Breaking the concept into manageable pieces, professional branding statements explain:

- Your specialty — who you are

- Your service — what you do

- Your audience — who you do it for

- Your best characteristic — what you're known for

Retrieved from http://www.dummies.com/how-to/content/what-is-a-pro-fessional-branding-statement.html

FIRST STEPS: WHO ARE YOU?

One of the first steps to take when developing your brand it to spend time reflecting upon who you are. What are your core values and what do you stand for? Sounds simple doesn't it? Think of 3-4 words that describe who you are. Are you trustworthy? Do you value honesty above all else? Are you collaborative, creative or innovative and do you expect that from others? Is working on a team important to you? Do you have a good sense of humor? Spend some time to define you are and what you stand for? When you identify your core values you control what you want your brand to say about you.

Don't get overwhelmed with the amount of things you should or should not be doing to build your brand as an educational leader. Your most important takeaway from this exercise should be your knowledge of how important it is to be continually working on developing a positive branding image throughout your career. Focus on always doing good work as an educator and if you follow some very simple common sense protocols and strategies your efforts will result in a manageable professional brand. All of the pieces, who you are, what you do, who you do it for, and what you're known for will all come together into one positive professional brand.

GAME TACTIC

Use the pages that follow to help you determine your core values. Then take time to actually think about these values and how you incorporate them into your daily life and workplace environment. Then target a few that you really want to work on.

IDENTIFYING YOUR VALUES

Circle Your Top 7 Personal Values

Accountability	Entrepreneurial	Listening
Achievement	Environmental	Making a difference
Adaptability	Efficiency	Open communication
Ambition	Ethics	Openness
Attitude	Excellence	Patience
Awareness	Fairness	Perseverance
Balance (home/work)	Family	Professional Growth
Being the best	Financial stability	Personal fulfillment
Caring	Forgiveness	Personal growth
Coaching Mentoring	Friendships	Power
Commitment	Future generations	Recognition
Community Involvement	Generosity	Reliability
Compassion	Health	Respect
Competence	Honesty	Responsibility
Conflict Resolution	Humility	Risk-taking
Continuous learning	Humor/fun	Safety
Cooperation	Independence	Self-discipline
Courage	Integrity	Success
Creativity	Initiative	Teamwork
Dialogue	Intuition	Trust
Ease with uncertainty	Job security	Vision
Enthusiasm	Leadership	Wisdom

FIRST STEPS IN DEVELOPING YOUR BRAND: WHO ARE YOU?

Choose your top three values from the seven you originally chose above. Start to examine why these are so important to you. Completing this activity will help you think more about how these values influence your actions and understand why you may respond in a certain manner. What are your core values and what do you stand for?

From the 7 values chosen, think about 3 that are most important to you. Write them in the spaces below.	Why do you believe this value is important to you?	Recall a moment in your life when you really lived this value. What behaviors did you exhibit that support this value?	How might you react if this value was not honored by others? Describe your feelings, thoughts and actions.
1.			
2.			
3.			

IMPROVE YOUR BRAND

Areas of Strength: Keep Doing

1.	4.
2.	5.
3.	6.

Areas of Improvement : Make a Plan

AREA: FOCUS GOAL	STRATEGIES
1.	
2.	
3.	
4.	
5.	

GAME TACTIC

Final Exam

Take this true/false test to assess your Promotion Quotient.

_____ 1.   Educational Administration is one of the fastest growing careers nationwide.

_____ 2.   Deciding to become a school administrator is an easy thing.

_____ 3.   You should not worry about applying for a job that has a long commute because you can always quit after a year.

_____ 4.   Mentors are important in the job search especially when interviewing.

_____ 5.   If you are a school principal you should only tell your secretary and lead teacher that you are applying for a new job.

_____ 6.   You should only include recommendations from people that say good things about you.

_____ 7. Try to secure letters of recommendation from people throughout your career.

_____ 8. It's okay to aggrandize your accomplishments a bit on a resume.

_____ 9. The letter of application, letter of introduction, and letter of intent are all the same thing.

_____ 10. All letters of introduction should explain why you are applying.

_____ 11. All letters of introduction should detail your hobbies and personal information.

_____ 12. The resume is a tool with one main purpose: Win an interview.

_____ 13. A resume should not be a history or list of your current or past job duties.

_____ 14. Winning resumes are written by the candidate.

_____ 15. A winning resume should convince the employer you have what it takes to be successful in this new career position.

_____ 16. A tagline can replace the resume objective with a statement about your expertise or vision as a leader.

_____ 17. Many people try to squeeze their resume onto one page and as a result delete important information.

_____ 18.   Design is not important in a resume.

_____ 19.   It is not that critical to address different district needs since they are all alike now.

_____ 20.   As you create your resume compose your headings and prioritize them by importance, impressiveness and relevance to the job you want.

_____ 21.   One typo is okay on a resume or letter of intent but more than that is not acceptable.

_____ 22.   Be sure to include your date of birth on your resume.

_____ 23.   You should be prepared for the first interview question, but don't memorize it.

_____ 24.   You can ask about salary in the interview if they ask if you have any questions.

_____ 25.   Don't stress out too much about what to wear for an interview. Best advice is to dress conservatively, be comfortable and look like a school administrator on his or her best day.

_____ 26.   Women should not wear Easter egg colors for an interview.

_____ 27.   If you show up to the interview with a black eye or on crutches don't tell the panel why.

_____ 28.   If you are late for the interview, school people are really nice and will usually give you a new time.

_____ 29. If you show up early to an interview, get to the lobby as soon as possible to check out your competition.

_____ 30. Interview panels want to know your decision making ability, your personality, your skills and if they like you.

_____ 31. Always thank the interview panel for the opportunity to interview first before launching into the first question.

_____ 32. Ninety-nine percent of all applicants recover from being nervous after the first question in an interview.

_____ 33. To find out how you're doing in the interview, ask the panel after answering a question, "Did I get that right?"

_____ 34. If you are asked a question that renders you speechless, pause and collect yourself. Don't point out any personal weaknesses.

_____ 35. Keep your answers to less than three minutes each.

_____ 36. If you can't answer a particular question tell the panel you have no experience or knowledge in that area but are a fast learner and know how to find the information to address that issue.

_____ 37. There are no 'right' or 'wrong' answers in an interview, just various degrees of good and bad responses.

_____ 38. It's important to talk about students in an interview.

_____ 39. Leave your portfolio at home; the interview panel wants to see and talk to you.

_____   40.   It's a good tactic to visit the community of the school district before interviewing so you can bring up something positive about their district in the interview.

_____   41.   Interview panel members want to see the real you... so using slang (Kiddos, alrighty guys) is a good idea.

_____   42.   If you are coming in second after interviewing, consider yourself in good shape in the promotion process.

_____   43.   You should give up after losing out on 4-5 job opportunities.

_____   44.   Many Human Resource officers will agree to meet with you to review your interview if you call and ask for an appointment.

_____   45.   Getting a new job can be more difficult than keeping or doing your current job.

APPENDIX

Sample Resume

RICHARD N. GREEN

4290 White Ave. ◆ Irvine, California 92618 ◆ 949-392-7769 ◆ rgreen@gmail.com

LEADERSHIP QUALIFICATIONS

Student focused, instructional leader known for being an energetic and caring professional with twenty-four years of experience. Proven track record of building high functioning teams and working through technical and sensitive issues with great results. Collaborative decision maker and master working under pressure, researching facts while soliciting input from all stakeholders.

PROFESSIONAL EXPERIENCE

HIGH SCHOOL PRINCIPAL 2012-present
Harbor High School, California Unified School District, Irvine, CA

Significantly improved student achievement through best practices in instruction and leadership; Harbor High School improved 30 API points over the last two years.

Developed an Instructional Action Plan with a focus on direct instruction, five instructional non-negotiables, and a rigorous accountability system resulting in over 600 formal, written teacher observations each semester.

Implemented Professional Learning Communities as evidenced by 100% of teachers participating on a bi-weekly basis, resulting in 13 of 15 subject CST subject test improvement the first year of operation.

Successfully prioritized and planned a $1.6 million site instructional and categorical budget emphasizing a positive impact on student achievement.

Conducted a human resource needs analysis for a staff of 150 with an annual personnel budget of over $6.5 million.

Successfully launched CLUB 350, a STAR recognition and rewards program, that provides incentives to students earning proficient or advanced on any CST subject test resulting in 1,400 students receiving special recognition and rewards.

Spearheaded several school-to-home communication systems including phone and text systems and launched a parent portal for attendance and grades in real time.

Served twice as Chairperson for Western Association of Schools and Colleges school review resulting successful accreditation.

Worked alongside the superintendent to promote EveryDay Counts, a student attendance program, resulting in 3% increased student attendance over a two year period.

Worked closely with the superintendent on a Transportation Task Force resulting in coordinated bell schedules, instructional minutes, and routes to ensure student safety and maximum utilization of instructional time.

Reorganized administration to connect each student to a single instructional leader/mentor.

Participated in at least two community events each week to establish and maintain strong community partnerships within the Orange County area.

Evaluated and improved the Advanced Placement Program resulting in increased passing rates from 22% in 2012; 44% in 2013; and 48% in 2014. Increased A.P. testing participation rate from 235 students in 2012 to 350 in 2015.

- Served as the secondary school representative on the Superintendent's Cabinet.
- Created the Eminence Program to provide targeted intervention for admitted student users of illegal drugs. Supervised a volunteer drug testing program at the school.
- Served as a key member of the Bond Oversight Committee successfully passing a $110 million general obligation bond.
- Collaborated with the district team to write and receive a $250,000 grant resulting in a web based credit retrieval system to increase graduation rates.

ASSISTANT PRINCIPAL 2008-2012
Shasta High School, Shasta Unified School District, Shasta, CA

- Initiated an instructional action plan emphasizing a teacher demonstration and modeling system.
- Created a discipline committee to drive policy changes that included all stakeholders.
- Fine-tuned the discipline system resulting in decreased discipline referrals.
- Spearheaded a co-curricular student code of conduct to cover all student groups.
- Refined graduation processes resulting in a dignified and respectful pubic celebration.

TEACHER-HEAD FOOTBALL COACH 2000-2008
Shasta High School, Shasta Unified School District, Shasta, CA

- Taught social science and special education.
- Participated in WASC leadership committee.
- Senior class advisor; responsible for graduation, baccalaureate, senior activities.
- Coached three sports resulting in 17 league championships, four section finalists, two section champions.
- Recognized five times as league coach of the year.

TEACHER-COACH 1995-2000
Sanger High School, Sanger Unified School District, Sanger, CA

- Implemented skill based instructional criteria for Industrial Technology areas of Electronics and Metal Shop.
- Coach of J.V. Football and Girls Basketball.

RELATED EXPERIENCE

Youth Counselor/Speaker/Resource Developer
Student Ministries Inc.

- Recruited students throughout Southern California for Conferences and Retreats
- Public speaker to student and adult groups of up to 150.
- Resource developer resulting in being the number one producer in the nation.

EDuCATION

Fresno Pacific University, 1996, Fresno, CA
Educational Administration

California Lutheran University, 1992, Thousand Oaks, CA
Master of Science, Counseling and Guidance

California State University, 1900, Fresno, CA
Bachelor of Arts

CREDENTIALS

California Clear Administrative Services Credential

California Clear Pupil Personnel Services Credential

California Clear Secondary Teaching Credential (Social Studies, Industrial Technology, Special Education and Resource Specialist)

ADDITIONAL PROFESSIONAL TRAINING

- WASC Visitation Training: Orange County Office of Education
- Accelerating the Achievement of English Learners
- Exemplary Practices in Educational Leadership: Doug Reeves
- California League of High Schools: Accelerating Student Achievement-Marzano
- Professional Learning Communities at Work: Rick DuFour
- Verify Students Are Learning: Data Works-John Hollingsworth
- California League of High Schools: Rick DuFour
- Getting Serious About School Reform: Robert Marzano Institute

ACTIVITIES/PROFESSIONAL ASSOCIATIONS

- Association of California School Administrators
- Association for Supervision and Curriculum Development
- California League of High Schools
- Principal's Partnership
- Tri-River Athletic Conference Executive Committee
- African Theological Seminary, Kitale Kenya. Guest Lecturer

HONORS AND AWARDS

2015 CSBA State Golden Bell Award Winner for Industrial Technology

ACSA Secondary Principal of the Year

F.F.A. Regional Golden Award for Service in Administration

Five time Sequoia League "Coach of the Year"

Orange County "Coach of the Year"

PRESENTATIONS AND STAFF DEVELOPMENT

Grades: Toxic Practices (Doug Reeves)

Professional Learning Communities: Looking Behind The Curtain (Rick DuFour)

Explicit Direct Instruction: The Power of TAPPLE (John Hollingsworth)

Student Learning Forum: Data, Instruction and Outcomes

Direct Instruction: Five Steps of Success

PROFESSIONAL REFERENCES

Bob Smith, Superintendent
Orange County Schools
(562) 265-3010

Maria Carillo, Superintendent
California Unified School District
(760) 855-8311

Chris Jones, Assistant Superintendent
Irvine Unified School District
(Cell (949) 217-4707

Mike Duarte, Board of Trustees
California Unified School District
(760) 855-4045

Sue Mott, Director Secondary Schools
Orange Unified School District
(949) 274-4700 x. 147

Rev. Blake Slater, Pastor
Orange Community Church
(562) 855-2313

Sample Interview Questions for Educational Leaders

IMPORTANT: *Use items from your completed scrimmage notes to guide your responses.*

1. Please give us a brief overview of your academic and professional background and why you are interested in this position.

2. You have read our brochure and know something about us. Tell us what you know about our vision and how you could impact this vision.

3. Can you tell us 1-2 successful experiences on which you can draw from to bring to this district?

4. Describe some strategies in the decision-making process that you would use.

5. What kinds of decisions would you share with the board?

6. What would you use as a process for developing and monitoring a budget?

7. How would you provide accountability for the district's finance?

8. How do you see technology fitting into our district?

9. What kind of leadership style do you use?

10. How do you communicate?

11. How have you involved the community in the decision making process. How do you communicate decisions?

12. Describe your experiences with diversity and how you have exercised leadership in this area.

13. Please describe your relationship with unions. How have you handled a difficult situation and your experience with contract negotiations?

14. What is your personal philosophy about the collective bargaining process, and how should it be approached by the district?

15. What do you envision as the major changes in public education over the next 5-10 years? How would you prepare us for these changes?

16. Given the increased emphasis on accountability and high stakes testing, how would you address less quantifiable outcomes such as student's social emotional intelligence and well-being?

17. If a site visit is made to your district, what three programs would you especially like the team to see and why?

18. Good employee relations are important to this board. Please tell us what steps you would take as a new (principal, director, superintendent) to establish a positive climate with all employees?

19. Please list the characteristics of a successful administrator and describe the components of an evaluation program for them. How would you assess whether they achieved the desirable characteristics and any assistance plan you would include to improve their skills?

20. What steps would you take to implement a new program or change an existing one in the district?

21. How will you delegate authority, assign responsibility, and maintain accountability. Please give us a couple of examples.

22. What is a good (principal, director, superintendent)? What professional skills and knowledge do you think a (principal, director, superintendent) should possess?

23. Describe four successful educational programs you have implemented?

24. What is your weakness?

25. What is your personal vision for a good school?

26. What can you do for us?

27. How far would you go to fight for your beliefs?

28. What process would you use to help a school district establish priorities?

29. How would you evaluate the instructional program to determine if we are delivering what we say we deliver?

30. As a (principal, director, superintendent) what would be the first goals that you would set for yourself?

31. What should be the role of a (principal, director, superintendent) in curriculum development and how would you monitor the coordination of the preschool-12 program?

32. How can we save costs on the special education encroachment? Special education costs are exorbitant. Talk to us about how we can curtail this expense.

33. How have you been involved in a community partnership? Describe a collaborative partnership.

34. What are the key factors that indicate a district is meeting the needs of all students and what methods would you take to insure continued academic improvement?

35. What Accountability Systems would you put in place in the district?

36. What experiences have you had with strategic planning? Define a successful strategic planning process.

37. Discuss a program that you have evaluated.

38. How do you resolve conflicts?

39. How do you define an outstanding School district?

40. How do you build trust?

41. How do you provide for English language learners?

42. What do you believe are the benefits of shared decision making?

43. How do you involve parents in schools?

44. What kinds of decisions have you made with facilities management?

45. What is your experience with PLCs?

46. What do you have left to learn?

47. What kinds of things do you do for your own professional development?

48. How do you inspire others to be the best that they can be?

49. How do you work with special interest groups?

50. There is always something coming from the state, how do you handle that?

51. What are your feelings about the state's accountability system?

52. What do you look for in a teacher?

53. What experiences do you have in career technical education?

54. How have you supported best practices in education based on research?

55. How do you identify, select, develop, supervise and evaluate staff?

56. How have you worked to address declining enrollment?

57. How would you determine priorities for cutting the budget? During a period of a decline in resources and revenues, please explain how you as a (principal, director, superintendent) would reallocate resources to add new programs and maintain facilities.

58. How would you get every child to read at grade level?

59. How have you improved school climate or safe schools?

60. What issues do you consider before adopting a program?

61. What does a quality staff development program look like?

Resume Power Words

LED A PROJECT

Chaired	Headed	Oversaw
Controlled	Operated	Planned
Coordinated	Orchestrated	Produced
Executed	Organized	Programmed

ENVISIONED AND BROUGHT A PROJECT TO LIFE

Administered	Founded	Incorporated
Built	Engineered	Initiated
Charted	Established	Instituted
Created	Formalized	Introduced
Designed	Formed	Launched
Developed	Formulated	Pioneered
Devised	Implemented	Spearheaded

SAVED TIME OR MONEY

Conserved	Deducted	Reconciled
Consolidated	Diagnosed	Reduced
Decreased	Lessened	Yielded

INCREASED EFFICIENCY, REVENUE, OR CUSTOMER SATISFACTION

Accelerate	Enhanced	Maximized
Achieved	Expanded	Outpaced
Advanced	Expedited	Stimulated
Amplified	Furthered	Sustained
Boosted	Gained	
Capitalized	Generated Improved	
Delivered	Lifted	

CHANGED OR IMPROVED SOMETHING

Centralized	Redesigned	Revitalized
Clarified	Refined	Simplified
Converted	Refocused	Standardized
Customized	Rehabilitated	Streamlined
Influenced	Remodeled	Strengthened
Integrated	Reorganized	Updated
Merged	Replaced	Upgraded
Modified	Restructured	Transformed
Overhauled	Revamped	

MANAGED A TEAM

Aligned	Hired	Shaped
Cultivated	Inspired	Supervised
Directed	Mentored	Taught
Enabled	Mobilized	Trained
Facilitated	Motivated	Unified
Fostered	Recruited	United
Guided	Regulated	

BROUGHT IN PARTNERS, FUNDING, OR RESOURCES

Acquired	Navigated	Partnered
Forged	Negotiated	Secured

SUPPORTED

Advised	Coached	Fielded
Advocated	Consulted	Informed
Arbitrated	Educated	Resolved

ANALYZED OR RESEARCHED

Analyzed	Audited	Evaluated
Assembled	Calculated	Examined
Assessed	Discovered	Explored

Forecasted	Mapped	Surveyed
Identified	Measured	Tested
Interpreted	Qualified	Tracked
Investigated	Quantified	

WROTE OR COMMUNICATED

Authored	Counseled	Lobbied
Briefed	Corresponded	Persuaded
Campaigned	Critiqued	Promoted
Co-authored	Defined	Publicized
Composed	Documented	Reviewed
Conveyed	Edited	
Convinced	Illustrated	

OVERSAW OR REGULATED

Authorized	Enforced	Monitored
Blocked	Ensured	Screened
Delegated	Inspected	Scrutinized
Dispatched	Itemized	Verified

ACHIEVED SOMETHING

Attained	Earned	Showcased
Awarded	Exceeded	Succeeded
Completed	Outperformed	Surpassed
Demonstrated	Reached	Targeted

*Adapted from the Muse (Retrieved from https://www.themuse.com/advice/185-powerful-verbs-that-will-make-your-resume-awesome).

Final Exam Answer Key

1. TRUE	2. FALSE	3. FALSE	4. TRUE	5. FALSE
6. TRUE	7. TRUE	8. FALSE	9. TRUE	10.TRUE
11.FALSE	12.TRUE	13.TRUE	14.TRUE	15.TRUE
16.TRUE	17.TRUE	18.FALSE	19.FALSE	20.TRUE
21.FALSE	22.FALSE	23.TRUE	24.FALSE	25.TRUE
26.TRUE	27.FALSE	28.FALSE	29.FALSE	30.TRUE
31.TRUE	32.TRUE	33.FALSE	34.TRUE	35.TRUE
36.TRUE	37.TRUE	38.TRUE	39.TRUE	40.TRUE
41.FALSE	42.TRUE	43.FALSE	44.TRUE	45.TRUE

Worthy Career Websites

RESUME GENIUS

https://resumegenius.com/how-to-write-a-resume

GLASSDOOR

https://www.glassdoor.com/blog/guide/how-to-write-a-resume/

TOPRESUME

https://www.topresume.com/career-advice/
make-a-great-resume-with-no-work-experience

THEMUSE

https://www.themuse.com/advice/
how-to-answer-the-31-most-common-interview-questions

EXPERIS

https://www.experisjobs.us/exp_us/en/career-advice/20-tips-job-interviews.htm

Made in United States
North Haven, CT
07 June 2022

At last—an educational leader reveals her inside tips and trade secrets to help you create a self-promotion plan, excel at the interview process, and win job offers.

Praise for Rules of the Game

Dr. Ryder's book was pivotal in securing my next position.
—Dr. Marylou K. Wilson

Rules of the Game was a perfect companion in helping me move from a principal to the Director of Secondary Education... Dr. Ryder provided excellent tips and insights and helped me land the first job I applied for!
—Dr. Melanie Dobson

I am a superintendent because I followed the exact steps and excellent advice outlined in Dr. Ryder's book.
—Dr. Laurie Goodman

Marilou Ryder, Ed.D. was recognized as the Johns Hopkins Outstanding Administrator of the Year, California Administrator of the Year and Fresno's Top Ten Business Professional Women of the Year. Marilou speaks regularly on the topic of career advancement for educational leaders. Dr. Ryder is a recognized authority in the field of executive mentoring and currently serves as an Associate Professor in the doctoral program of organizational leadership for Brandman University, part of the Chapman University system.

Author of **The SeXX Factor** *and* **92 Tips from the Trenches**

ISBN 9780990410348

90000

9 780990 410348

R.T. Floyd

Manual of Structural Kinesiology

Nineteenth Edition

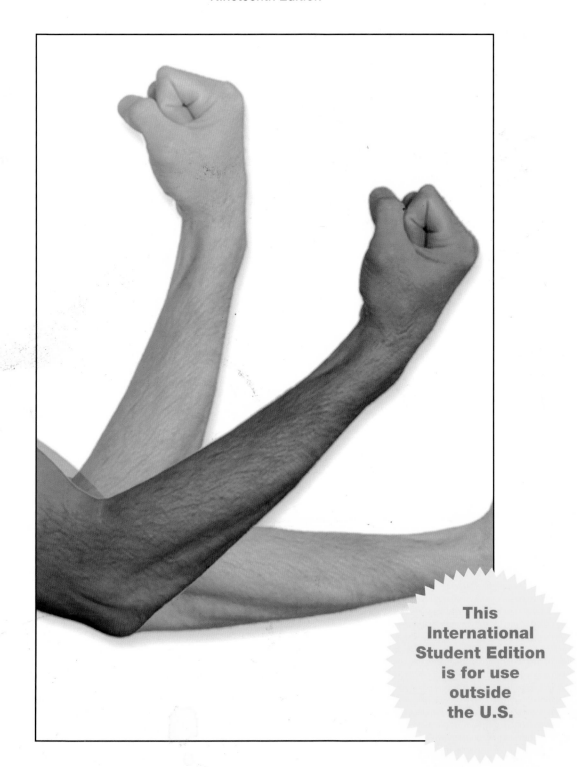

McGRAW-HILL INTERNATIONAL EDITION